GA
CEN_____ _____

Drama for Students, Volume 9

Staff

Editorial: Ira Mark Milne, *Editor.* Elizabeth Bellalouna, Elizabeth Bodenmiller, Angela Y. Jones, Michael L. LaBlanc, Polly Rapp, *Contributing Editors.* Dwayne D. Hayes, *Managing Editor.*

Research: Victoria B. Cariappa, *Research Team Manager.* Cheryl Warnock, *Research Specialist.* Corrine A. Boland, Tamara Nott, Tracie A. Richardson, *Research Associates.* Timothy Lehnerer, Patricia Love, *Research Assistants.*

Permissions: Maria Franklin, *Permissions Manager.* Margaret A. Chamberlain, Edna Hedblad, *Permissions Specialists.* Erin Bealmear, *Permissions Associate.* Sandra K. Gore, *Permissions Assistant.*

Production: Mary Beth Trimper, *Production Director.* Evi Seoud, *Assistant Production*

Manager. Stacy Melson, *Production Assistant.*

Imaging and Multimedia Content Team: Randy Bassett, *Image Database Supervisor.* Robert Duncan, *Imaging Specialist.* Michael Logusz, *Graphic Artist.* Pamela A. Reed, *Imaging Coordinator.* Dean Dauphinais, Robyn V. Young, *Senior Image Editors.* Kelly A. Quin, *Image Editor.*

Product Design Team: Cynthia Baldwin, *Product Design Manager.* Pamela A. E. Galbreath, *Senior Art Director.* Gary Leach, *Graphic Artist.*

© 2000 Gale Group
27500 Drake Rd.
Farmington Hills, MI 48331-3535

Gale Group and Design is a trademark used herein under license.

ISBN 0-7876-4083-2
ISSN 1094-9232

Printed in the United States of America
10 9 8 7 6 5 4 3 2 1

Lady Windermere's Fan

Oscar Wilde

1892

Introduction

Lady Windermere's Fan was Oscar Wilde's first produced play, and it was an instant success on the London stage. Chronicling a series of misunderstandings and deceptions in the high society world of Victorian London, critics and audiences alike were charmed by Wilde's trademark wit and intelligence.

In the play, Lady Windermere considers leaving her husband of two years when she believes he's been unfaithful with a woman—who turns out to be her own mother. Remarkably, it will be the mother who sets her straight without ever revealing her identity.

In his letters, Wilde claimed that he did not want the play to be viewed as "a mere question of pantomime and clowning"; he was interested in the piece as a psychological study. Although the play has been deemed outdated by recent critics, *Lady Windermere's Fan* continues to entertain audiences all over the world.

Author Biography

In 1854 Oscar Wilde was born in Dublin to affluent parents. His father was a prominent surgeon and archaeologist; his mother was a witty poet, Irish nationalist, and feminist.

Wilde excelled at the Portola Royal school and then at Trinity College, where he took the Gold Medal for Greek. In 1878 he won a scholarship to Magdalen College at Oxford.

Wilde attracted a crowd of admirers for his witty, intellectual lectures and his outrageous cult of "aestheticism." He believed in art-for-art's-sake, a philosophy he had learned from his association with John Ruskin, an art critic and Oxford don.

A very successful lecture tour of America in the early 1880s on "The Principles of Aestheticism" earned him much-needed income as well as an international reputation.

His marriage to Constance Mary Lloyd in 1884 produced two children; it was during this time he wrote his best works: *The Picture of Dorian Gray* (1891), *Lady Windermere's Fan* (1892), *A Woman of No Importance* (1893), *An Ideal Husband* (1895), and *The Importance of Being Earnest* (1895).

These works brought him financial success and the admiration of the literary circles. His reputation as an insightful, witty, and urbane playwright was established worldwide.

In the early 1890s, at the peak of his career, Wilde entered into a destructive romantic relationship with Lord Alfred Douglas, nicknamed "Bosie." After Bosie's disapproving father, Lord Queensbeery, insulted Wilde, the playwright foolishly sued for defamation of character. Queensbeery's return suit for "depravity" resulted in Wilde's conviction for sodomy—and a two-year jail sentence.

After serving his sentence, Wilde emerged from jail bankrupt, scandalized, and spiritually bereft. He lived alone in France until his death from cerebral meningitis in 1900. His remains are buried in Paris.

Plot Summary

Act One

The play opens in Lady Margaret Windermere's home, where she is arranging roses for a party later that evening in celebration of her birthday. Lord Darlington visits, and Margaret chides him for flirting with her. He contends that a woman whose husband of two years is unfaithful has a right to "console herself."

Lady Windermere fails to recognize his oblique reference to her husband, and calls herself a Puritan with "hard and fast rules" for fidelity. Lord Darlington continues to flirt with her, but she ignores him.

He leaves and the Duchess of Berwick and her daughter, Lady Agatha Carlisle, enter. The Duchess cattily reports that Lord Windermere has been spending time and money on a Mrs. Erlynne, whose social status is questionable. The Duchess admits that her own husband has had his "little aberrations," and assumes all men are immoral.

Yet the Duchess is anxious to marry off her daughter Agatha, saying "a mother who doesn't part with a daughter every season has no real affection."

After they depart, Lady Windermere looks through her husband's desk and discovers payments to Mrs. Erlynne in his secret bankbook. When he comes in and finds her looking at it, he gets angry. He demands that his wife invite Mrs. Erlynne to their party in order to help the woman back into society. Lady Windermere flatly refuses.

He addresses an invitation to Mrs. Erlynne himself. Outraged, Lady Windermere threatens to hit the infamous woman with her new birthday fan when she arrives. Lord Windermere protests and she storms offstage.

As the curtain drops, he agonizes over what to do about the situation. Apparently there is something to his relationship with Mrs. Erlynne, for he groans "I dare not tell her who this woman really is. The shame would kill her."

Act Two

The Windermere's party is in full swing, and the guests are being announced. The Duchess of Berwick has advised Agatha to dance with Mr. Hopper of Australia, a prospective suitor.

Lord Augustus Lorton, brother of the Duchess, asks Lord Windermere how Mrs. Erlynne can gain respectability. It seems that Lorton hopes to marry her. He is reassured by her invitation to tonight's ball, for it paves her way into "this demmed thing called society."

Mrs. Erlynne appears and smoothly makes her way from guest to guest, especially the men. Their wives glare indignantly. In the meantime, Lady Windermere remains cold to her husband, and seeks comfort from Lord Darlington, who takes advantage of her mood by confessing his love and offering to take her away.

At first shocked, Margaret asks for time to see if her husband would return to her. Defeated, Lord Darlington announces that he will leave England the next day and bids her goodbye.

As the music stops and guests come back into the room, the Duchess of Berwick talks approvingly of Mrs. Erlynne to Margaret, yet advises her to get her husband away from the woman.

Agatha whispers to her mother that Mr. Hopper has proposed. With her goal in hand, the Duchess now takes full charge, insisting that the couple remain in London rather than return to Hopper's home in Sydney.

Two gentlemen offer alternate views to Mrs. Erlynne's presence at the ball: one says that Lady Windermere must have "common sense," while the other credits Lord Windermere with cleverly hiding his indiscretion in the open.

Mrs. Erlynne informs Lord Windermere that Lord Lorton has proposed; in addition, he has asked for 2000 to 2500 pounds a year from him. Annoyed but compliant, Windermere exits with her to the terrace to discuss the details.

As the music strikes up again, Lady Windermere decides to run away with Lord Darlington and leave her husband. She leaves a farewell letter on her desk. Mrs. Erlynne enters and reads it.

She lies to Windermere about the letter's contents and calls for her carriage. Lord Augustus enters with a bouquet for Mrs. Erlynne and proposes. Without responding, she instructs him to take Windermere to his club until morning, and he complies.

Act Three

Alone in Lord Darlington's rooms, Lady Windermere vacillates between staying and going back to her husband. When Mrs. Erlynne arrives, Margaret recoils in contempt of her rival. Mrs. Erlynne pleads with her to return to her husband, denying any relationship with him.

Lady Windermere is moved when Mrs. Erlynne reminds her of her duty to her child. She tearfully decides to go home, but upon hearing voices, they both hide behind the curtains. Lord Augustus ("Tuppy" to his friends), Lord Darlington, Dumby, Cecil Graham, and Lord Windermere arrive, having been turned out of the club.

The men speak cynically of women and society as they settle into a game of cards. This scene displays Wilde's wit as the men banter back and forth. Then Cecil sees Lady Windermere's fan on a table. He shows it to Tuppy for a chuckle at Darlington, who has been moralizing, for apparently he has a woman in his rooms.

Windermere's reaction to seeing his wife's fan,

however, is dramatic. He threatens to search Darlington's rooms. Darlington refuses. Only the sudden appearance of Mrs. Erlynne, stepping out from behind the curtain, stops a probable fight. She pretends to having taken Lady Windermere's fan by mistake. The men respond variously with contempt, astonishment, and mockery, as the curtain falls.

Act Four

Back at home, Lady Windermere lies on a sofa, wondering why Mrs. Erlynne disgraced herself to save her reputation. Lord Windermere comes in and sympathetically suggests a visit to the country. He also expresses a change of heart about Mrs. Erlynne, whom he now considers "as bad as a woman can be."

His wife defends her and insists on seeing her once more before they depart. Lady Windermere almost confesses the truth, but Parker interrupts them. He is carrying Lady Windermere's lost fan and Mrs. Erlynne's card on a tray. Margaret tells Parker to invite her up, in spite of her husband's protest.

Mrs. Erlynne enters, and apologizes for taking the fan. She announces that she is leaving England and wants a photograph of Margaret with her child. While Lady Windermere goes upstairs to find one, Lord Windermere confronts Mrs. Erlynne for causing his first quarrel with his wife, and for misrepresenting herself. It is revealed to the audience that Mrs. Erlynne is Margaret's long-lost mother.

It is true that Mrs. Erlynne had been extorting money from him, but she has had a change of heart, too. She fails to convince him of her new sincerity, but revels in her new relationship with her daughter —who never learns that Mrs. Erlynne is her mother.

Before leaving, Mrs. Erlynne offers Lady Windermere a piece of advice: not to tell Arthur of nearly leaving him. Lord Augustus arrives and accepts Mrs. Erlynne's explanation that she was only looking for him at Darlington's home. He proposes to her again. Margaret comments that he is, indeed, "marrying a very good woman."

Characters

Agatha

Agatha is the daughter of the Duchess of Berwick. She is passive and only interested in getting married.

Lady Carlisle

See Agatha

Caroline

See Lady Jedburgh

Mrs. Cowper-Cowper

Mrs. Cowper-Cowper is one of the society ladies who attends Lady Windermere's ball.

Lord Darlington

Lord Darlington is in love with Lady Windermere, and hints of her husband's apparent infidelity in order to gain her affection. When she does not return his love, he leaves town.

Duchess of Berwick

A manipulative woman, the Duchess of Berwick thrives on the pettiness of high society. She is the one who initiates the series of misunderstandings between Mrs. Erlynne and Lady Windermere by gossiping about Mrs. Erlynne and Lord Windermere.

At the same time, she masterfully orchestrates the marriage of her daughter to Mr. Hopper, an Australian visitor. Once she snags the young man, she begins her next project of making sure the new couple stays in London rather than going to Sydney.

Margaret Erlynne

The mysterious Mrs. Erlynne is Lady Windermere's long-lost mother—a fact that is not revealed until the late in the play. Lady Windermere never learns her true identity.

Mrs. Erlynne wants desperately to be accepted within her daughter's social circles. She has a reputation as a woman with a shady past, a "divorced woman, going about under an assumed name, a bad woman preying upon life." In other words, she seems to be a woman with no substantial income, and therefore no right to socialize with the Windermeres and their circle.

However, Mrs. Erlynne reveals herself to be a woman of quality, who puts aside her own interests in favor of protecting her child. Having found herself capable of a mother's devotion, she decides to escape in order to spare her daughter further embarrassment. Fortunately, Lord Lorton still loves her and offers his hand in marriage.

Cecil Graham

Cecil Graham is a cynic who trades witty barbs with his pals Windermere, Dumby, and Lorton. He is described as the experienced man about town. He is the one who discovers Lady Windermere's fan in Darlington's rooms.

Mr. Hopper

Mr. Hopper is an Australian man who proposes to Agatha. Although he hopes to take her home to Sydney, the Duchess wants them to remain in England.

Lady Jedburgh

Lady Jedburgh is Cecil Graham's dowager aunt.

Lord Augustus Lorton

The brother of the Duchess of Berwick, Tuppy is a rather simple fellow. He is in love with Mrs. Erlynne and is greatly relieved to learn that she has received an invitation to Lady Windermere's ball, since this serves as an invitation into high society.

He is a very trusting man; he accepts Mrs. Erlynne's excuses and does not rescind his marriage invitation after the scandal.

Parker

Parker is the Windermeres' butler.

Lady Plymdale

Lady Plymdale is the wife of Mr. Dunby. She disapproves of Mrs. Erlynne and of her husband's visits with her.

Rosalie

Rosalie is Lady's Windermere's maid.

Lady Stutfield

One of the society ladies who enjoy the social season.

Tuppy

See Lord Augustus Lorton

Lord Arthur Windermere

For most of the play, it seems that Lord Windermere is having an affair with Mrs. Erlynne. Like his wife, Windermere is a sincere and generous person. He is also loyal: even when it is in his self-interest to tell his wife the truth, he keeps Mrs. Erlynne's secret. His goodness and straightforward manner is symbolized by his plain way of talking.

Lady Margaret Windermere

Margaret is a beautiful, intelligent, and honorable woman who nearly leaves her husband because of a vicious rumor. At first, she rebuffs Lord Darlington's advances and believes that her husband is not having an affair with Mrs. Erlynne. However, she prepares to leave her husband when it appears that the gossip about her husband's relationship with Mrs. Erlynne is true.

Media Adaptations

- *Lady Windemere's Fan* has been adapted in two silent films: a 1917 version by Ideal Film, and a 1925 Warner Brothers production called *The Fan* by director Ernest Lubitsch.

- Otto Preminger remade *The Fan* with sound in 1949.

- Librettist Don Allan Clayton

adapted the play for an Off-Broadway musical comedy called *A Delightful Season* in 1960.

- A recording of the play exists in a 1997 audiotape version with Michael Sheen speaking the part of Lord Darlington.

Hypocrisy

Hypocrisy can be defined as pretending to be something one is not or feigning to believe in something one does not. Most of the characters in Wilde's play accept hypocrisy as a necessary component of their social world. People in high society must pretend, must conform to the social norm in order to maintain their position. Hypocrisy is the glue that holds together a complex web of relationships; if the truth were to come out, these relationships would fall apart.

Lies are a necessary tool to avoid conflict. For example, Dumby agrees with Mrs. Stutfield that the season has been "delightful," and in the next breath agrees with the Duchess of Berwick that it has been "dreadfully dull." Likewise, the Duchess of Berwick tells Lady Windermere that her nieces never gossip, then later declares that they always gossip.

Topics for Further Study

- Explore and discuss the role of wit in *Lady Windemere's Fan*. Is it necessary to the play's meaning? Why or why not?

- Is Mrs. Erlynne a "good woman?" Support your answer with evidence of her deeds and words.

- Research the genre of "comedy of manners." What are the characteristics of such a play? Can you think of a recent play or movie in that genre?

- Could such a situation as that in *Lady Windemere's Fan* happen today? Write an essay describing what you would change to make the situation more modern.

Hypocrisy is distinguished from virtuous lies, which are told to protect someone else. To ease the comfort of others—even though this might require lying—was part of the upper class code of conduct. Encouraged by Tuppy's remark that women with a past are "demmed interesting to talk to," Lord Windermere withholds the truth of Mrs. Erlynne's past in order to protect his friend from a truth that would ruin his marriage plans.

Mrs. Erlynne rises above hypocrisy when she sacrifices her own reputation for her daughter's. Although she has lived a life of hypocrisy, and she is desperately trying to get back into the society that once rejected her, she throws it away out of love.

The Bad Mother

The role of women was changing in Victorian society. Women were seeking greater independence, and they were entering the workforce in increasing numbers. The suffragist movement attracted many supporters, as women petitioned for the rights to vote and to own property (any money or property of the wife belonged to her husband upon marriage).

This greater independence for women was opposed on all fronts: politically, socially, and culturally. Soon, the independent woman was being portrayed as a bad wife and a bad mother.

Many plays, stories, poems, and articles featured the image of the "bad mother": the woman who abandons her children to pursue some selfish interest, such as a love affair or career. Such entrepreneurial social behavior was portrayed as dangerous and threatening to society in general.

Wilde's play is unusual for its time in allowing the "bad mother," Mrs. Erlynne, to make peace with her daughter (although without recognition of her motherhood) and to pursue her own life.

Screen Scene

A *screen scene* is a scene in which an actor hides behind a drape or furniture and overhears the other actors. Melodrama, with its emphasis on secrets and their revelation, often makes use of the screen scene to allow a character to discover a secret. This discovery is a turning point in the plot.

In *Lady Windermere's Fan,* Lady Windermere's eavesdropping convinces her of her husband's fidelity. Also Mrs. Erlynne's sacrifice of her own reputation convinces her of the older woman's virtue.

Part of the purpose of the screen scene is to allow a character to discover information he or she is not supposed to hear. At the same time, the risk of being discovered in the act of eavesdropping adds to the dramatic intensity of the scene.

Further adding to the dramatic intensity, the play often has the eavesdropper leave something behind in the room. The other characters see and recognize a glove, a fan, or other personal item. Only a clever diversion such as that undertaken by Mrs. Erlynne can prevent the eavesdropper from exposure.

Comedy of Manners

During the Restoration period (1660–1699), fashionable audiences flocked to comedies that poked fun at the foibles and witticisms of high society. Pompous characters were held up for ridicule as they indulged in the misbehaviors and pretensions of the sophisticated set.

During the Victorian era, more serious plays came into style. Therefore, Wilde's comedy of manners was a refreshing change of style that revitalized comedy and set the stage for modern comic theatre.

Compare & Contrast

- **Victorian London:** Industrialization leads to a migration from the country to towns and cities as thousands of workers toil in British factories.
  Today: More and more workers are part of the "service" and high-tech economy as opposed to manufacturing and industry. It is more economical to build factories in Third World countries.

- **Victorian London:** The railroad revolutionizes travel as well as the movement of raw materials and finished goods. The middle and working class could afford excursions to seaside resorts and to the towns and cities for entertainment.

Today: The Internet puts information and entertainment into the hands of a computer-literate society. From art and literature to stock trading and shopping, the Internet offers many options for its users. People gather in virtual chat rooms instead of drawing rooms, parlors, and music halls.

- **Victorian London:** The mail is delivered up to three times per day in London. For those who could afford it, a message could be sent across town in the morning and a response received that evening.

  Today: People can send messages instantaneously by phone, electronic mail, instant messaging, and teleconferencing.

Aestheticism Movement

The late nineteenth century "art-for-art's-sake" movement was promulgated by Walter Pater (1839–1894), an Oxford don who tutored Oscar Wilde. Wilde became a living example of his teacher's theory, which placed style and beauty above moral and social responsibility. Wilde's adherence to this theory earned him the name "The Great Aesthete."

According to Pater, the aesthete appreciated beautiful things and beautiful literature. Interest in art was facilitated by the rise in leisure time for the upper and middle class. The middle class adopted the values of the upper class and viewed the appreciation of art as part of their social training.

The aestheticism and Pre-Raphaelite movements opposed the Victorian obsession with industry, engineering, and efficiency. When Oscar Wilde declared to customs officials in America that "I have nothing to declare but my genius," he alluded to the refinement of character that he nurtured for its own sake.

Wilde surrounded himself with art and sought to exemplify Walter Pater's concept of the true critic, one with "a certain kind of temperament, the power of being deeply moved by the presence of beautiful objects." Pater looked to the Renaissance era for a model of obsession with style.

Aesthetics valued the completely innocent person, such as the character Dorian Gray in Wilde's novel, *The Picture of Dorian Gray* (1891). Gray was both pure and physically beautiful until corrupted by an older man.

Lady Windermere is another beautiful and simple character with a natural ability to appreciate art and true sentiment.

Victorian Society

Three years before Oscar Wilde's birth, England celebrated the triumphs of industry in The Great Exhibition of 1851, which was housed in the magnificent Crystal Palace. Inside, observers viewed the highest technical achievement of every nation, and England's contributions put her in the forefront of scientific achievement.

The exhibition demonstrated the benefits of progress. England was at the height of prosperity, with income increasing exponentially through the efficiencies of industrialization. With a growing economy, a burgeoning middle class began to aspire to the fashions and habits of high society.

By the end of the nineteenth century, the newly affluent class was beginning to shoulder its way into formerly forbidden regions—in politics, clubs, and the workplace.

It was also a time of budding feminism, as women took more and more aggressive steps to win suffrage. In the magazine he edited for two years, *The Women's World,* Wilde ran articles by women on both sides of the women's suffrage issue. Wilde had also changed the title from *The Lady's World* out of respect for the blurring lines between social classes.

Critical Overview

Wilde's *Lady Windermere's Fan* garnered much popular and critical controversy on its debut at the St. James Theatre in February 20, 1892. The audience was filled to capacity with the literary stars of the time: Frank Harris, Henry James, actress Lillie Langtry, and a host of critics.

However, according to Vyvyan Holland in the introduction to *The Complete Works of Oscar Wilde,* Wilde caused a furor of resentment when he came onto the stage with a cigarette in his gloved hand and his signature green carnation in his lapel and told the audience,

> Ladies and Gentlemen. I have enjoyed this evening *immensely.* The actors have given us a *charming* rendition of a *delightful* play, and your appreciation has been *most* intelligent. I congratulate you on the *great* success of your performance, which persuades me that you think *almost* as highly of the play as I do.

The reviews the next morning focused on the playwright's impertinence. Beckson states that Clement Scott accused Wilde of "condescension" and trying to "take greater liberties with the public than any author who ha[d] ever preceded [him] in history."

In an interview, Wilde took full responsibility for deviating from the expected humility of the author: "I have altered all that. The artist cannot be degraded into the servant of the public: humility is for the hypocrite, modesty for the incompetent. Assertion is at once the duty and the privilege of the artist."

The play ran for five months, then made a tour of the provinces and returned to London for another successful run. Although Henry James called the performance "infantine. . . both in subject and form," George Bernard Shaw, who had not yet made his name in theater, admired it.

Beckson declares that A. B. Walkley maintained that the "plot is always thin," that it is "full of... glaring faults" but was nevertheless a "good" play. Those who enjoyed the plethora of witty epigrams compared Wilde to Congreve and Sheridan, even though, in Wilde's play, "all the men talk like Mr. Oscar Wilde."

The play was produced a year later in New York City by Maurice Barrymore, but Wilde was not happy with the production because Lord Darlington was presented as a villain—not as a person intent on saving Lady Windermere from an unfaithful husband. The New York production ran for several successful months.

More recent critics have explored gender issues relating to Wilde's homosexuality. Only recently Wilde's plays have been treated as separate from his personal life.

The deconstructionist view (of the 1970s and 1980s) perceived an inversion of the Victorian melodramatic conventions. Others have focused on the possible influences on his work.

Lady Windermere's Fan, with its somewhat outdated concern for the errant mother and its staging requirements (actors capable of sophisticated social banter and elaborate costumes and sets), is not often produced today. It is viewed as a period piece.

What Do I Read Next?

- Richard Sheridan's *The School for Scandal* (1777) is a comedy of manners concerning a wife who nearly betrays her older husband.

- Henrik Ibsen's *A Doll's House* (1879) depicts a mother who feels constrained and unhappy in her limited role. As a result, she leaves her husband and children.

- *Mrs. Warren's Profession* (1898), written by George Bernard Shaw, views the theme of the wayward mother with marked parallels to Wilde's play.

- A play by Moises Kaufman about Wilde's trial for homosexuality, *Gross Indecencies: The Three Trials of Oscar Wilde,* offers insights into Wilde and the social world of Victorian London.

Sources

Beckson, Karl, ed. *Oscar Wilde: The Critical Heritage,* Alfred A. Knopf, 1970, 434 p.

Wilde, Oscar. *The Complete Works of Oscar Wilde; with an introduction by Vyvyan Holland,* Harper & Row, 1989 (1966).

Further Reading

Bloom, Harold, ed. *Oscar Wilde,* Chelsea House, 1985, 146 p.

> An anthology of recent scholarship on Wilde, with a brief commentary by Bloom in which he concerns himself with the "anxiety of influence" (Bloom's term for a writer's struggle to create something fresh and new) in Wilde.

Coakley, Davis. *Oscar Wilde: The Importance of Being Irish,* Town House, 1995, 246 p.

> Explores the role of the Irish raconteur in Wilde's family and in his social life.

Ellman, Richard. *Oscar Wilde,* Alfred A. Knopf, 1988, 632 p.

> The definitive Wilde biography.

Freedman, Jonathan. *Oscar Wilde: A Collection of Critical Essays,* Prentice-Hall, 1995, 257 p.

> Essays, brief biography, and selected bibliography.

Holland, Vyvyan Beresford. *Oscar Wilde: A Pictorial Biography,* Viking Press, 1960, 144 p.

> An intimate biography written by Oscar Wilde's son.

Knox, Melissa. *Oscar Wilde: A Long and Lovely Suicide,* Yale University Press, 1994, 185 p.

> A psychoanalytic biography that explore Wilde's childhood experiences and their effect on his later life.

McCormack, Jerusha, ed. *Wilde the Irishman,* Yale University Press, 1998, 205 p.

> Essays on aspects of Wilde's works.

Powell, Kerry. *Oscar Wilde and the Theatre of the 1890s,* Cambridge University Press, 1990, 204 p.

> Places Wilde into a literary and historical context.

Raby, Peter, ed. *Cambridge Companion to Oscar Wilde,* Cambridge University Press, 1997, 307 p.

> Examines the defining themes of Wilde's work.

Lightning Source UK Ltd.
Milton Keynes UK
UKHW02f0947190818
327463UK00009B/229/P

9 781375 383110